Why do we need a
Temple?

Chaitanya Charan Das

BE, COEP

Readers interested in the subject matter of this book
are invited to correspond at the following address:
Sales Manager:
Krishnakishore das
A-102, Bharati Vihar, Katraj, Pune – 411 046
Tel: +91-98224-51260
Email: krishnakishoredas@gmail.com
　　　　voicebooks@voicepune.com

Vedic Oasis for Inspiration, Culture & Education (VOICE)

Head Office: Sr. No-50, Katraj Kondhwa Bypass Road,
Opp to Shatrunjay Temple, Kondhwa Budruk,
Pune-411048. Tel: +91-86050-36000

Branch Office: 4, Tarapore Road, Next to Dastur Boys' School,
Camp, Pune 411001. Tel: +91-20-41033210

Email: voicebooks@voicepune.com,
　　　　ccd.rnsm@gmail.com
Website: www.thespiritualscientist.com

© 2009 Chaitanya Charan Das
All rights reserved with the author

Previous printing: 10000 copies
Third printing: Mar 2014, 5000 copies

This book is dedicated to

His Divine Grace
A.C. Bhaktivedanta Swami Srila Prabhupada,
Founder-acharya,
International Society for Krishna Consciousness
(ISKCON),
who, by his determination and vigor, built 108 temples all over the world, and who, by his vision and compassion, transformed these temples into "a house in which the whole world can live."

&

To all of you, the readers, my brothers and sisters in the one family of our Divine Father. I hope and pray that this small book will help you discover the peace, the joy, the vitality and the maturity, which we are all looking for in life and which a temple can help us find.

Contents

TRANQUILITY..................3

EDUCATION...................7

MEDICATION................17

PURIFICATION.............36

LOVE..............................55

ENGAGEMENT..............69

Why do we need a temple?

Ratan Gupta (**RG**) is a wealthy industrialist, well-known for being charitable to noble causes. He recently attended an ISKCON program at a friend's house, where the speaker Sanatana Swami (**SS**), a venerable monk who has been teaching God consciousness for the last 35 years, invited him to visit the local ISKCON temple. One early evening, Ratan decides to go to the temple. As he parks his car outside the temple, he notices hoardings depicting a grand new temple that ISKCON is planning to build. He enters the temple, has darshan and enquires about Santana Swami. He is directed to a small room, where he sees the effulgent Swamiji sitting erect on the floor behind a small table. The room is filled with pictures of Krishna on the walls and books about Krishna in the shelves. Sanatana Swami greets him with a warm smile and invites him to take a seat. Their conversation:

RG: Pranam, Swamiji.

SS: Hare Krishna, Guptaji. Please accept the blessings of Lord Krishna. We are happy that you have taken time out from your busy schedule to visit our temple. Did you have darshan?

RG: Yes, the Lord is so beautifully dressed and decorated. I heard you are coming up with a new temple.

SS: Yes. Krishna willing, the temple will be constructed in two years if the funds come regularly.

RG: That brings me to a question that has been in my mind for a long time. Can I ask you?

SS: Certainly.

RG: Do we need such costly temples? So many people are suffering without food, clothing, shelter. Isn't that a much more urgent necessity for society than an expensive temple?

SS: Certainly it saddens our heart to see people suffering without the basic necessities of life. Many humanitarian organizations are working to help them and much more can be done. At the same time, a temple plays a vital role in the integration and the development of the entire community, a role that is not being played at all in our modern society.

RG (*surprised*)**:** Really? What is that role?

SS: I will briefly explain the social services provided by a temple through an acronym **T.E.M.P.L.E.**

T – **T**ranquility

E – **E**ducation

M – **M**edication

P – **P**urification

L – **L**ove

E – **E**ngagement

RG: Sounds interesting.

TRANQUILITY

SS: Just as food, clothing and shelter are the basic needs of the body; peace is a basic need of the mind. Today, there is practically no system to provide for this basic mental need. Worse still, our fast-paced, stress-filled lifestyle agitates our mind a lot. No wonder the

World Health Organization (WHO) has declared that the greatest medical challenge of the current century will be not AIDS or cancer but mental health problems. The temple is one of the few places where one can immediately experience a deep peace just by going into the premises.

RG (*looking thoughtful*)**:** When I entered the temple I was wondering how it is such a haven of serenity despite geographically being amidst the hustle-bustle of the city. Where does this tranquility come from?

SS: The tranquility is a natural result of the divine vibrations that constantly pervade a temple. Those vibrations result from both the presence of the Lord in His deity form as well as the  constant chanting of His holy names. Many, many people come to the temple in the evening to de-stress themselves before returning home. They take darshan of the deities, attend the arti or sit in the temple hall taking in the divine atmosphere. Thus they become mentally recharged to cope with the challenges of life.

The founder-acharya of ISKCON, His Divine Grace A.C. Bhaktivedanta Swami Srila Prabhupada, wanted to have temples right in the hearts of the cities so that maximum number of people would have easy, quick access to the tranquility that the temple offers.

RG: Sometimes I wonder whether peace of mind is a luxury that we can ill afford when we have so many duties to perform for our family, office and society.

SS: Peace of mind is not a luxury, but is a necessity that enables us to perform our duties sustainably. To lift a 5 kg weight for a few minutes is not difficult. But if we were to lift it continuously for the 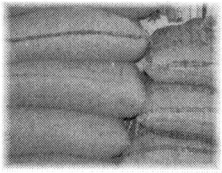 rest of our lives, it would soon become a burden, an unbearable burden. We would need to relieve ourselves of the weight by short breaks that would allow the muscles of our arm to rest and regain strength. Similarly our duties – and the anxieties that inevitably come with them – are like burdens on our minds. If we let these burdens weigh on our minds constantly, they exhaust us mentally. We need short breaks that allow our minds to rest and regain strength.

People try to get these breaks through entertainment – by watching TV and movies. Entertainment may sometimes refresh us, but often it leaves us with more agitating thoughts, desires and memories.

On the other hand, when we come to the temple, we take those mental burdens off and sooth our minds with the healing serenity that pervades the temple. Then when we are mentally rested and refreshed, we restart our duties with greater effectiveness.

In fact, because people don't take such nourishing breaks, they become ineffective in their personal functioning and irritable in their interpersonal dealings, leading to so many avoidable problems.

RG: I had never thought of the temple contributing to society by providing mental rest.

SS: You are not alone in that. I too had hardly any idea of the value of our culture till I came in contact with ISKCON, And I would surmise the same holds true for most Indians, including even those Indians who are proud of their culture. That's what makes the next contribution of the temple to society – education – so vitally important. Many temples offer a tranquil atmosphere, but ISKCON temples particularly offer spiritual education too.

EDUCATION

RG (*somewhat skeptically*)**:** Spiritual education? Do we really need that, especially in this age of science?

SS: Science tells us how to do things, but spirituality alone teaches us why to do things. For example, the medical colleges teach how to cure a patient, but they don't teach 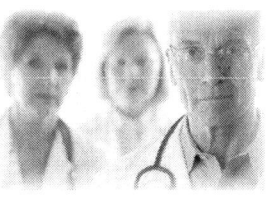 why to cure him. Consequently, many doctors see their patients as money minting machines and often subject them to needless tests and treatments so as to earn more out of them. Similarly, in every profession, when the motive of earning takes primacy, professionals end up exploiting their clients.

RG (*protesting*): But that is a human defect. Why blame education for that?

SS: The purpose of real education is not just to train students in technical skills, but also to rectify the lower human tendencies. Sadly, modern education fails to do that. Learning is not just for earning, but for service.

RG (*thoughtfully*)**:** Service?

SS: Yes, the doctor's real duty should be to serve the patients, to free them from their pains and to heal them. Think of how much better our world would be if everyone were working to serve each other, not exploit each other. Spiritual education can create that culture of service.

RG: Why do we need spiritual education for that? We just need to help people understand the need to be good and to do good to others.

SS: Without spiritual education, most people will not be able to stay good or do good for a long time; they would soon succumb to an immoral, exploitative mentality.

RG: Why?

SS: Being good and doing good or living by moral principles is like following traffic laws for smooth and safe travel. The purpose of travel, however, is not merely to follow the laws but to reach the destination. If a traveler feels that the traffic laws delay or obstruct his reaching the destination or that there's no policeman to catch him, he will soon become tempted to break the laws.

Like traffic laws, moral principles promote order, specifically orderly social interactions. But modern education doesn't teach us about the goal of social transactions or the goal of life itself. So, most people choose by default the incessantly glamorized goals of modern consumerist society—wealth, enjoyment, prestige, power, possession, position. The Bhagavad-gita, which has been acknowledged as a philosophical masterpiece by Emerson, Einstein, Gandhi and many other thinkers worldwide, explains graphically how such a materialistic worldview leads to corruption and degradation. When the social culture aggressively propagates materialistic goals and education does nothing to counter this propaganda, then morality appears unnecessary and even undesirable, resulting in the mentality: "If the goal of life is to earn money and enjoy life, then why be honest, when honesty will severely limit my earning and enjoyment? By hook or crook, earn and enjoy. There's no God in front of whom I have to account for my deeds; there's only this one life for me to enjoy. I just have to make sure that whatever I do, I do it cleverly enough to not get caught."

RG (*thoughtfully*): Yes, the resolve for morality doesn't last. In my thirty years of business experience, I have seen many moralists glide down to immorality.

SS (*nodding*): More the materialistic propaganda spreads, more the immorality increases – and not just in earning, but also in every form of enjoyment. According to the US Congressional Quarterly, in the 1960s, the top disciplinary problems in US schools were sticking gum under school

desks, noise during classes, breach of dress code, littering the classroom and running in halls. Now, the top disciplinary problems in US schools are drugs, alcohol, pregnancy, suicide, rape, robbery and assaults on teachers. And as India is becoming westernized, soon these problems will come here also.

RG (*nodding gravely*)**:** It's scary when we hear about incidents like students shooting co-students and teachers as happened in Virginia Tech a few years ago. But how can spiritual education counter this?

SS: Ultimately, everyone is seeking happiness. Spiritual education helps us understand where to find the highest happiness. Most people seek materialistic happiness, but such happiness is always temporary; we have to lose it all at the time of death – and sometimes even earlier. Moreover, even that temporary happiness is illusory. The Bhagavad-gita explains that we are not our material bodies, but are spiritual beings, souls. We are temporarily occupying material bodies, which are like our vehicles. Satisfying the body by material enjoyment is nothing more than giving fuel to the car. Just as car fuel cannot satisfy the car driver, material enjoyment cannot satisfy the soul and so it is essentially illusory. And worse still, even this illusory happiness always brings misery with it. The Mahabharata explains that before we acquire material pleasure, we hanker for it; when we acquire it, we worry  about losing it; when we inevitably lose it, we lament over the loss. We can summarize the nature of material enjoyment by the acronym TIME: **T**emporary **I**llusory **M**iserable **E**njoyment.

RG: That's quite a sobering analysis.

SS: Spiritual education doesn't stop with condemning material happiness; it also points the way to a better form of happiness, a source of happiness that can never be taken away from us. The Vedic texts explain that as souls, we all have an eternal loving relationship with the all-attractive Supreme Lord. In loving and serving God, we can relish supreme and everlasting happiness; the more we love God, the happier we become. The scriptures of the other great religions like Christianity and Islam also describe love of God as the ultimate goal of life. Hence, love of God is the nonsectarian, universal, spiritual goal of life.

RG (*thoughtfully*)**:** Love for God as the ultimate goal of life? Isn't that too other-worldly and impractical? And how does that lead to morality?

SS: Love for God certainly directs our vision to the other world, the eternal spiritual world beyond the temporary material world. But this other-worldly goal does not make us impractical; rather, it builds the most solid foundation for living practically in this world. Just as when we switch on the master switch in a house, all the lights in the house automatically  turn on, love for God similarly results in love for all living beings. We realize that all of us are brothers and sisters in the one universal family of God. When we love all living beings, we no longer desire to exploit or manipulate others for our selfish interests. Instead, our love for God inspires us to love and serve each other. This creates a culture of warmth, trust and service, which encourages moral behavior. This contrasts sharply with the modern culture of alienation, suspicion and exploitation, which fosters immorality.

When we follow a genuine spiritual path, even in its early stages, it triggers our inborn value system. We intuitively realize that God is our greatest well-wisher and that the rules He has made for us are in our ultimate interest. So we voluntarily and lovingly choose to lead a life of moral and spiritual integrity, as ordained by God. And as we find inner happiness by loving God, we become freed from selfish, lusty, greedy, and egoistic drives. No longer do we feel we are missing something because of our morality. Morality ceases to be the "difficult but right" choice. Rather we choose morality as the natural path to our spiritual growth.

This is how spiritual education leads to the culture of service, by which people can constructively use all other education for doing good to others. Without spiritual education, people often abuse their material education to exploit others.

RG (*after a thoughtful pause*)**:** My grandparents used to tell me that in their times, they would leave the doors of their houses open and still no one would steal anything. Now I get some idea of how that was possible.

SS: Yes. In Vedic culture, even uneducated peasants would hesitate to sin because they were aware of the law of karma: for every one of our actions, we will have to endure a corresponding reaction, sooner or later. And this awareness would be spread by the temple, which served like a university for systematic spiritual education. Unfortunately, over the centuries, this emphasis on spiritual education was lost; the culture remained, but the philosophy explaining the purpose of the culture became inaccessible to most people. Consequently, nowadays millions of people visit temples without obtaining any idea about the ultimate goal of life.

To counter this spiritual ignorance, Srila Prabhupada established right from the beginning of ISKCON in 1966 a culture of regular classes. In our temples, we now have a daily morning class on the Srimad Bhagavatam and a daily evening class on the Bhagavad-gita. Additionally, in the evenings, devotees conduct systematic courses on the Bhagavad-gita in the temple as well as in several other parts of the city in which the temple is located. These courses lead students from the basics of spirituality like scientific, logical proof for the existence of the soul and God to advanced principles like analysis of the identity and the personal nature of God. Our temples also have a weekly satsang program every Sunday,  where hundreds of people come to the temple for a spiritual get-together comprising of a discourse, kirtan and Prasad for everyone. And the results are there for everyone to see. Connected with this temple itself, there are over two thousand people who, by receiving spiritual education, have started leading pure lives free from all bad habits and centered around service to God and all His children. Similarly, all over the world, over one million ISKCON devotees have received spiritual education and have started living service-oriented lives.

RG: That's impressive. Do you think that everyone can become spiritually-minded?

SS: Why not? Every one of us is potentially divine,

no matter what our current condition is. We just have to reactivate that divine nature. The temple not only helps remove our ignorance of our divine nature, but also teaches the practical process to heal the diseased mentality that has resulted from the ignorance. Thus a temple is not just like a university offering education, but also a hospital offering medication.

MEDICATION

RG (*surprised*)**:** A hospital offering medication? What sort of medication?

SS: From the spiritual viewpoint, all improper, immoral behaviors are the symptoms of a diseased mentality. The Vedic scriptures explain that this diseased mentality is caused by six main germs: lust, anger, greed, envy, pride and illusion. Let's see how these breed most criminal behaviors. Lust causes rapes and sex-related crimes; greed causes corruption and financial transgressions; and anger causes terrorism and violent crimes. Similarly, millions of people worldwide squander billions of dollars on self-destructive indulgences like smoking, drinking and drug addiction. What makes them addicted to substances that poison and kill their own bodies? The lust for instant pleasure. Thus the infections of the mind cause people to harm others and harm even themselves, thus leading to major global problems.

The Vedic scriptures also explain that remembrance of God is the cure to these infections of the mind. We are basically pleasure-seeking creatures. When we seek pleasure externally, the germs enter into our mind and infect us, for they all promise us external pleasure. But the remembrance of God gives us inner happiness and thus frees us from the infection of these germs. The easiest way to remember God is by chanting his holy names. Hence, the holy name of God is the medicine to cure this diseased mentality. Let me share how Srila Prabhupada administered the medication of the holy name with astonishing results.

Srila Prabhupada went to America in the 1960s at the advanced age of seventy and found himself amidst the counterculture of the hippies. The hippies were young people who had rejected the established values and norms of society and expressed their stance through unconventional clothing and behavior. The hippies had rejected mainstream society as aimless, and mainstream society had rejected the hippies as useless. But Srila Prabhupada taught these hippies the ultimate aim of life, healed them of their drug addiction and other bad habits by training them in chanting the holy names and elevated them from ignorant self-destruction to enlightened self-realization. This transformation of hippies into "happies" was nothing short of a miracle. The US government, despite all its national resources comprising of hospitals, doctors, social welfare plans and social workers, had come to its wits end about how to change or even tackle the hippies. But Srila Prabhuapda, a solitary, elderly man with no material resources, transformed them by his spirituality and his compassion. That's why an eminent US scholar Professor Stillson Judah, Professor, Graduate Theological Union Library, Berkeley University, noted, "A.C. Bhaktivedanta

Swami has the remarkable ability to turn drug-addicted hippies into devotees of Krishna (God) and servants of mankind."

Just think if we could cure the lust, anger and greed in the criminals, the crime rate would drop dramatically and significant national resources would become available for purposes more constructive than law enforcement. Similarly, if we could cure addicts of their addictions, just think of how those billions of dollars could be channelized for the good of the world.

RG (*doubtfully*): This sounds too good to be true. Firstly, changing the habits of criminals and addicts is no easy task; old habits die hard. Secondly, many of these people don't even want to change.

SS: Yes, healing the diseased mentality is not easy especially if the disease is in an advanced stage as in the case of criminals and addicts. But we should not underestimate th power of God's mercy as manifested in His holy name. By God's grace, what is ordinarily impossible becomes entirely possible.

ISKCON has a prison preaching ministry in India,

America and several other countries. I could tell you many stories of incredible, curative transformations that chanting has brought about. Let me share just one story of a person who was both an addict and a criminal.

Chris Matthews, a youth from Atlanta, USA, started taking morphine in 1986 due to the pressures of youth. Gradually it became an addiction. To get money for his compulsive drug needs, he started robbing people and stores in 1992. While robbing a shop in 1993, he took a heavy overdose and fell unconscious. On regaining consciousness, he found himself in a prison  hospital. He came to know that the shop owner had called the police, the police had rushed him to a nearby prison hospital and the doctors had battled for hours to get him out of the jaws of death. In 1994, he was tried and sentenced to eight years imprisonment. Heartbroken at being separated from his recently-wed wife, he resolved he would never have anything to do with God henceforth in his life. Soon, however, he realized that the withdrawal pains and the physical and mental rigors of prison life would be impossible to endure without some spiritual solace. In USA the crime rate has been spiraling unabatedly for several decades and the expenditure of the US government on prisons is astronomical. Secular efforts to reform prisoners have met with hardly any success, so the US government allows its prisoners to attend reformation programs conducted by various spiritual organizations. Chris attended classes on Christianity, Buddhism, Kabbala, Sufism, Islam – whatever was accessible in the prison, but nothing helped. After two years of fruitless groping, from the innermost core of his heart, he offered a fervent prayer to God, begging for help.

No sincere prayer ever goes unheard. Within days after the prayer, he came in touch with an ISKCON prison minister, who mailed him a copy of Bhagavad Gita As It Is. His physical hardship, mental agony and spiritual searching combined to make him a ripe candidate for enlightenment. From his very first reading, he felt as if he was being revived by a breath of fresh air. He could perceive the eternal truths within the message of the

Gita: I am a not the body, but the soul; I am suffering in material existence due to my forgetfulness of God. This forgetfulness can be easily cured by chanting the holy names of God.

Chris soon started chanting the holy name of God, specifically the maha mantra: Hare Krishna Hare Krishna Krishna Krishna Hare Hare, Hare Rama Hare Rama Rama Rama Hare Hare. Within a short time he became free from his addiction. In fact, though he was physically within the prison walls, he felt himself more free in spirit than he had felt ever before in his life because he was no longer shackled and tormented by self-destructive desires. Within the prison itself he became a vegetarian and started offering his food to the picture of Krishna in the Bhagavad-gita. He soon became inspired by his Gita study to start practicing nishkama karma yoga in the prison, doing his assignments in a detached dutiful devotional spirit. Not only did he experience complete release from his drug addiction, but he became so composed, integrated and self-satisfied that he emerged as a source of inspiration and solace for his fellow-prisoners. As he was released from prison, he returned home. After the initial courtesies, he started teaching his daughters chanting so as to equip them to protect themselves when they would enter the turbulent teenage years. Later on, he had a divine inspiration to share his good fortune with the many other souls who were languishing in the prisons of America and so he joined the ISKCON Atlanta prison ministry. Now the same Chris, who was formerly a hardened criminal, is now actively serving as a prison minister for numerous prisons in Atlanta, reforming many, many lives ravaged by crime. This is the kind of dramatic transformation that chanting can bring about – from prison to prison ministry, from prisoner to prison minister.

RG (*astounded*)**:** That's quite a story. Do you think this can happen with everyone?

SS: Why not? There is an old saying: "Every saint has a past; every sinner, a future." No one is incorrigible. If the infection is so deep as to have covered the victim's intelligence and conscience, then healing him will be difficult. But there are a significant number of criminals and addicts who want to become better human beings, but don't know how to change themselves. Even if we could help these people alone, that would make a significant difference in their lives and in our world.

And my thirty-five years of experience as a spiritual healer has shown me that chanting works, often beyond the wildest expectations, for all those who give it a sincere try. All serious ISKCON devotees practice the four regulative principles: no meat-eating, no gambling, no intoxication and no illicit sex. Before becoming devotees, some of them were habituated, even addicted, to these activities, but now they have become free. Thus they are living examples of the healing potency of the holy name.

RG: How does the chanting of the holy names have so much power? It seems to be such a simple activity.

SS: Out of His love for us, God manifests Himself as His holy name. The Padma Purana declares: "abhinnatvam nama naminoh", "There is no difference between the name of God and God Himself." So the holy name is no ordinary sound; it is God Himself.

Here's an example to illustrate how a thing can be much more valuable that what it appears to be. A mother tells her four year old child to tear and throw into the dustbin all paper that he finds fallen on the ground in their bedroom. The child gleefully gets down to work, tearing and throwing away the papers. Suddenly the mother notices a five hundred rupee note that had fallen from her husband's pocket as he rushed to office that morning. The child also notices that note and picks it up to tear it. The mother screams in alarm, "Stop." Taken aback, the child asks, "Did you not tell me tear all paper lying on the ground?" The mother hastily takes the note from his hand, keeps it safely in her purse and then replies, "But this is not ordinary paper." The child looks at the paper in surprise: it seems just like the papers that he has torn. Seeing his incredulity, the mother says, "With this paper, you can get five hundred chocolates for your birthday." And when he actually gets the chocolates from the shop, then he realizes that the five hundred rupee note is no ordinary paper.

Similarly, those with undeveloped spiritual consciousness think that the holy name is just like any ordinary sound. But when they chant the holy names themselves and experience profound peace and immense joy, then they understand that the holy name is different from any ordinary sound. For no ordinary material sound can bring such joy, just as no ordinary paper can get five hundred chocolates.

God, out of His unlimited love for us, makes Himself easily available to us in a portable form that we can literally carry on our tongue-tip. Srila Prabhupada would say that when we chant the holy name, the Lord dances on our tongues.

RG: Interesting. I have seen that you specifically chant the Hare Krishna mahamantra. What is the meaning of this particular mantra?

SS: The word mantra means 'manas trayate iti mantra'; mantra is that sound vibration which delivers the mind from anxieties and passions. Mahamantra refers to the great mantra, the one mantra that contains the potency of all other mantras. The mahamantra "Hare Krishna Hare Krishna Krishna Krishna Hare Hare / Hare Rama Hare Rama Rama Rama Hare Hare" contains three seed words Hare, Krishna and Rama. Krishna and Rama are names of God. Krishna refers to God's all-attractive nature and Rama refers to God's being the reservoir of all pleasure. Hara (changed to Hare in the vocative) is the name of the energy or the consort of God. All of us are children of God. So when we chant the holy names, we basically call out to our divine parents. The mood of this call is: "O Lord who is all-attractive, O Lord who is the reservoir of all pleasure, O energy of the Lord, please engage me in Your service."

As souls, it is our nature to lovingly serve God and experience supreme happiness therein. The germs in our minds impel us to act for our selfish enjoyment, independent of God's service. So, when we pray to be engaged in the Lord's service, we are also praying to be freed from those germs. Thus chanting is essentially a prayer to be restored to our natural, spiritually healthy condition.

RG: Is this chanting like meditation?

SS: Certainly; chanting is meditation in its highest form. The essence of meditation is not just to sit in a particular physical posture, but to take the mind off the changing and fix it on the unchanging. Our material positions and possessions – indeed, all the things of this world – keep changing, for change is the only thing constant in this world. But God is beyond all the changes of this world. So, the unchanging object of meditation is God. Just as a boat in an ocean is shaken by the waves, our mind is shaken by the ups and downs of life. Just as the flow of waves never ends, the ups and downs never end. And just as the boat is made steady when it is anchored, similarly the mind can be made steady 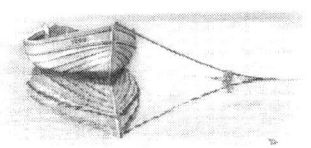 by fixing it on God. The easiest way to fix the mind on God is by chanting His holy name. Hence, in this age, meditation can be most easily and effectively done by chanting the holy names of God.

Chanting as a meditation can be done in two forms: as japa (individual meditation) and sankirtan (group meditation).

RG (*surprised*)**:** You mean to say that kirtan with its loud singing and energetic dancing is also a form of meditation?

SS: Yes. In fact, sankirtana, the congregational

chanting of the holy names of Krishna to the accompaniment of music and dance, is actually meditation in its most practical and joyful form. Let's see how.

As we discussed earlier, the purpose of meditation is to connect with and experience the unchanging spiritual reality. Silent meditation, as done through breathing exercises and yogic postures, tries to achieve this by negating the material, by deactivating the body and the mind. As the germs of the mind multiply through physical and mental activity, stopping activity checks the spread of infection. But since we're habituated to physical and mental activity, wouldn't it be easier and more natural if somehow the body and the mind could be used to connect ourselves with spiritual reality? That is precisely what sankirtana does. Engaging the body in graceful dance for the pleasure of the Lord, and the mind in prayerful contemplation on the sound of

His holy names quickly and joyfully transports us to spiritual consciousness.

Thus, sankirtana acts like spiritual-music therapy to heal the soul. Just as iron burdens the person carrying it, negative thoughts and emotions burden a person mentally. Sankirtana floods the heart with positive, precious, golden emotions like love, faith, and joy and flushes away negative, burdensome emotions like hatred, anxiety, and sorrow.

Lord Shri Chaitanya Mahaprabhu, who appeared some five hundred years ago, revived and popularized sankirtana all over India. Lord Chaitanya displayed divine dance so enchantingly that His golden complexion, graceful gait, and intense devotional emotions charmed everyone—from aristocrats like the king of Orissa down to hardened criminals.

Indeed, Lord Chaitanya's dance charmed even the

Muslim emperor Akbar, who lived half a century after the Lord. Akbar glorified Lord Chaitanya in these words: "Hail Thee, O Caitanya, the victor of my heart.... O my heart's Lord, how can I express the love I have for Thee? Shah Akbar craves a drop from the sea of Thy love and piety." (Quoted by D. C. Sen in Chaitanya and His Age) These verses composed by a Muslim emperor in glorification of one who is commonly considered a Hindu saint illustrate the universal appeal of sankirtan.

Shrila Prabhupada, as the most prominent modern proponent of Chaitanya Mahaprabhu's teachings, popularized the divine dance of sankirtana in our times. Chanting and dancing devotees are now a familiar sight in major cities all over the world. Given that dance, an exuberant physical activity, and meditation, an introspective spiritual activity, intersect in this simple-looking dance, it can well be called the ultimate dance-meditation.

RG (*impressed*): The devotees dancing gracefully on the streets is always a pleasing sight, but it's certainly innovative to think of that as the ultimate dance-meditation.... And that verse of Akbar is stunning.

SS: Yes. Chanting is universally appealing because it awakens our joyful spiritual nature. So bodily designations like "I am Hindu", "You are Muslim" or "He is an American" don't matter, for the soul is beyond all these bodily designations.  Indeed, when our devotees chant on the streets in various parts of the world, often many onlookers – whether they be Christians or Muslims or even nonbelievers – become spontaneously drawn to participate by clapping, waving and even dancing.

RG: Excuse me. Did you say that our religion is a bodily designation?

SS: Yes. The different religions are different means to raise our consciousness from the bodily to the spiritual level. But often followers of different religions neglect the ultimate purpose of their religious practices and merely identify themselves as belonging to the religion of their birth. Just the other day I was glancing through a book, where the author introduced himself as "a Jew atheist."

RG (*laughing*): "Jew atheist?" A Jew is one who follows the God of the Old Testament, so how can there be a Jew atheist? I get your point of religion becoming just another bodily designation.

SS: We do not preach to convert people from one religion to another; we preach to convert people from being materialists to being spiritualists, for that alone can heal them. Whenever I am invited to speak at interfaith meets, I encourage followers of other religions to chant the holy names as per their religious traditions so that they can be elevated from the material to the spiritual level. Of course, from Vedic scriptural verdict and objective observation, we can see that, in the present age, the quickest and best way to raise one's consciousness is the chanting of the Hare Krishna mahamantra. But we are not fanatical; all the names of God are potent and one can chant according to one's religious beliefs.

Coming back to our topic of meditation, japa can be done anywhere and everywhere, but we get the maximum healing effect if we can give exclusive attention to the holy name. So japa is best done in a quiet place in the peaceful early morning hours. And the temple provides a serene atmosphere for serious meditators to deeply absorb themselves in japa. In fact, in our temple, the early morning hours are reserved exclusively for meditational chanting of the holy names. If you visit our temple from 5:30 am to 7:30 am, you will see so many devotees, striving earnestly to absorb themselves in chanting.

And for sankirtan, the temple is the base. We have sankirtan in the temple periodically throughout the day. And from the temple, devotees go out to various neighboring parts of the city to perform public sankirtan. Everyone who hears the kirtan benefits from the spiritual vibrations of the holy names. Still, sankirtan done in front of the Deities is doubly purifying; we get purified both by the holy name and by the sacred darshan of the Deities.

RG (*hesitantly*)**:** Your talk about the Deities reminds me of a question I always wanted to ask. What exactly is the relationship between the Deity and God? Many people criticize Hindus as idol worshipers.

SS: What you have asked is an important question. And its answer leads us to the next benefit that the temple offers.

PURIFICATION

SS: Spiritual knowledge and practices are not meant only to make bad people good, but also to make good people better and better till they become the best they can be. The Bhagavad-gita (4.2) describes that its wisdom is especially meant for the leaders of society. In the Vedic times, the saintly kings led their lives and their kingdoms according to spiritual principles and thus took care of both the material and spiritual welfare of their citizens.

Purification is the key that unlocks the treasure of happiness locked in our own hearts. As spiritual beings, we are, by our very nature, sat-cit-ananda, eternal, full of knowledge and full of happiness. So the purer we become, the more we can experience our own joyful nature. When we are joyful within, then we interact with others to share our joy with them. But when we are empty within, we are inevitably craving for external pleasures. So, when we interact with others, then consciously or unconsciously, we tend to manipulate and exploit them to get what we want from them. In fact, when a person is in material consciousness, that is, seeking pleasure externally, his first default thought on meeting anyone is: "What can this person do for me?" On the contrary, when a person is in spiritual consciousness, that is, satisfied internally, his first default thought on meeting anyone is: "What can I do for this person?"

That's why it's vitally important for the leaders of society to be purified and satisfied internally, because otherwise they will soon become controlled by their lower natures. And once they become controlled by their lower natures, they have the power and the means to exploit others in a way that few other people have. So the real problem in the world is not a shortage of money, but a shortage of character and compassion among those with influence. In modern society, those with political and monetary power are especially influential. Just consider these staggering statistics:

According to an article in the Times of India on 22-5-08, the German government sent an official letter to the

Indian government stating that 70 lakh crore rupees of Indian money are lying in the Swiss bank. With this money, we can repay 13 times of our country's foreign debt. The interest alone can take care of the Centre's yearly budget. People need not pay any taxes and we can pay Rs.1 lakh to each of 45 crore poor families. India is often thought of as a poor country, but India is the undisputed champion in black money; in fact, Indian money in the Swiss bank exceeds the money put by all the other countries combined together!

If the wealthy and the powerful people worldwide became pure-hearted, then they would be motivated by compassion rather than greed and would use the resources that God has given them to do good to the world.

RG: It's eye-opening to know that an impure heart motivated by greed can cause problems of such magnitude or that a pure heart can make such a huge difference on a practical level.

SS: Yes. There's another important way in which purification can make a massive difference in society. When our hearts are pure, we can understand God's

Why do we need a temple? 39

plan to do good to the world and can harmonize our plans with His. Else even if we want to do good, if our plans run contrary to God's plan, we will end up causing more harm than good, despite our noble intentions. Let's understand this more clearly.

God, being the greatest well wisher of everyone, has a benevolent plan for every one of us individually and for the whole world collectively. The root cause of all problems in the world is twofold: man's forgetfulness of God's plan and man's vain attempt to impose 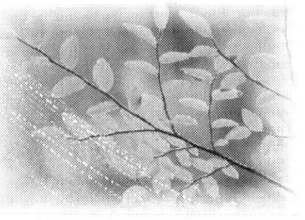 his own plan. For example, consider the environment. God has made a perfect plan for the ecology to cleanse and balance itself. We humans take in oxygen and give out carbon dioxide during our respiration. The plants counterbalance by taking in carbon dioxide and giving out oxygen during their photosynthesis. But we forgot God's plan for us to live in harmony with nature by simple living and high thinking. Instead, we imposed our own plan of mass industrialization and urbanization globally, and cut down trees indiscriminately, thus upsetting the delicate atmospheric balance. And we all know the consequences of that.

So the best use of human intelligence is to understand God's plan and the best use of human energy is to cooperate with and participate in His plan. And both these require a pure heart. God has endowed us humans with free will, so we can choose whether to cooperate with Him or not. If we are pure-hearted, we naturally choose to cooperate with him. Consequently, we become further purified, others become benefited and the world functions harmoniously. But if we are impure-hearted, we act according to the dictates of the germs in our mind and end up causing suffering to ourselves and to others. To save us from similar future suffering, God then unfolds an alternative plan aimed at reforming our errant, non-cooperative, impure mentality.

To help us make the best use of our free will, God has revealed His general plan in His words given in the Bhagavad-gita: All of us can attain the highest happiness in life if we live in harmony with God and nature, by molding our lives according to the principles He has given in the scriptures; by so doing, we can fully utilize our dormant talents and resources, do the greatest good to the world and can also ultimately return back to the kingdom of God to be eternally happy in divine love with Him.

To help us further in making right choices, God is also ready to guide us constantly and reveal His specific plan if we just tune ourselves to hear His loving, guiding voice within our own hearts. Unfortunately, when we are impure-hearted, the clamor of our material desires drowns out His voice. Nonetheless, we can still express our desire to cooperate with His plan by purifying our hearts and by chanting His holy names, which constitutes a prayer for serving Him. God promises in the Gita (10.10-11), "For those who serve Me with love, I purify their material desires, and give them the intelligence to understand and participate in My plan."

Thus, the seemingly simple act of chanting enables us to dramatically change our role in the divine plan for the world – from being a disruptor to being a contributor.

RG: Wow! I had never thought that the simple act of chanting has so much significance.

SS: The Vedic scriptures describe that only those who are willing to be led by God are qualified to become true leaders. Else they end up misdirecting or underutilizing human energy. Modern leaders define progress as "let's make things better", whereas Vedic spiritual leaders defined progress as "Let's make people better." Modern leaders emphasize technological development thinking that this will make people happy. But has it? Although we have far more technology than what we had a few centuries ago, we also have much more stress, depression, addiction, violence, crime and suicide than in earlier times.

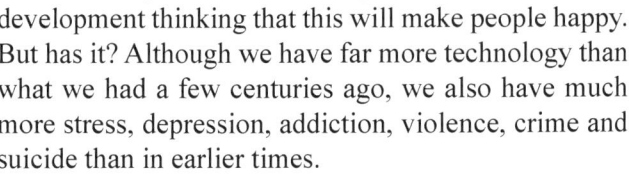

The Vedic leaders knew that real happiness comes from within, not from without. They knew that unless people made themselves better by purifying themselves, they would never become happy, no matter how much they achieved externally. That's why they would emphasize, by their word and by their personal example, purification of the heart so as to enable everyone to experience their own joyful spiritual nature. They would make it their top priority to visit temples every day, hear spiritual wisdom from saints, find time in their daily schedule for prayer and chanting and thus purify their own hearts. For example, King Kulashekhara, a famous saintly king of South India, would submit at the end of each working day a report of the day's activities in his court to the Deity. His mood was that the kingdom belonged to the Deity and that he was just a caretaker serving on behalf of the Lord.

This emphasis on inner development was a defining characteristic of Vedic leadership and that is still the emphasis of the devotees in the temple. So the temple is like a community from the past transported into the present that offers modern leaders a living example by studying which they can redefine their priorities. The temple is the place where leaders can learn and experience God's wisdom and love, purify their hearts and thus become inspired to lead in harmony with God's plan. And it can also be the place where future leaders can be trained to lead in harmony with God's plan. In the past, even the princes would go to the gurukula, which was an educational institute centered on a temple, to get training in character, devotion and compassion before they would take up their royal responsibilities.

RG: The temple as a training ground for leaders! That's an innovative idea…Sorry to change the topic, but we were discussing about the Deity.

SS: Yes, we are coming to that topic. The Deities along with the holy name are vital to any purificatory program. Till now we were discussing the importance of purification. Now let's discuss how purification actually takes place.

RG: Ok.

SS: God is supremely pure and supremely purifying. The Mahabharata confirms this: *pavitranam pavitram yo mangalanam ca mangalam.* The closer we go to Him, the purer we become. And the farther we go from Him, the more we become vulnerable to impurities. So the essence of any purificatory program is to bring us closer to God. But because we are presently living in material bodies and have material senses which can only perceive material things, we cannot perceive God, who is completely spiritual. So, how can we purify ourselves?

God makes Himself available to us through matter as the arca-vigraha (the worshippable Deity), a special manifestation made of the ashtadhatus, eight elements in which the Lord appears as the Deity. The Srimad Bhagavatam (11.27.12) states that these elements are stone, wood, metal, earth, paint, sand, the mind or jewels. Just as a currency note is different from ordinary paper, the Deity is different from ordinary stone. If the Lord can appear from a stone pillar as Narasimhadeva, why can He not convert matter into spirit and appear as the Deity to a devotee who wants to lovingly serve Him?

The Deity is different from an idol. The form of the Deity is made according to precise scriptural description, not according to someone's fanciful imagination. Srila Prabhupada would give the example of a post box. If someone puts up a red box outside his house and puts his mails in it, they will never reach the intended destination. But if a red box is authorized by the post office and one puts one's letters there, they are sure to reach their prescribed destination. Similarly, if one worships a form made according to one's own imagination, then worship of that form is not worship of God. But if one worships a Deity made according to scriptural descriptions, then such worship is authorized and so is factual worship of the Lord.

The full import of Deity worship is very deep and cannot be fully conveyed by any one analogy. Some people mistake the Deity to be an authorized *via media* by which one worships God who is actually beyond the Deity. But the scriptures declare that the Deity is God Himself.

RG: But the Deity is made of matter, whereas you yourself just said that God is spiritual. So how can the Deity be God?

SS: God being the controller of both matter and spirit has the ability to convert matter into spirit. He transmutes matter into spirit out of His unlimited love for us.

In our current material state of consciousness, we are greatly influenced by the impressions that come to us through our senses. Indeed, most impurities come in through our senses. Therefore, our contact with God will have the maximum purificatory effect if we could have sensory experience of God. That is precisely what the Deity offers us. We can see the Lord with our eyes; nay, our eyes can feast on His beautiful form. Further, just as the intimate servants of a king would serve him by dressing and feeding him, similarly the intimate servants of the Lord – the pujaris – serve the Lord by bathing, dressing, decorating and feeding Him.

The transmutation of matter into spirit is done through a special ceremony called *prana-pratistha*, during which the devotees pray to the Lord to appear as the Deity so that they can have the opportunity to serve Him. And the Lord reciprocates out of His love for the devotees and manifests Himself as the Deity.

RG: What you have said sets me thinking. Still, it seems difficult to accept that the Deity is God Himself and not just a representation of God.

SS: There is a way each one of us can experientially verify that the Deity is Krishna Himself.

RG (*eagerly*)**:** What is that?

SS: How can the child know that the paper he was about to tear is actually a five hundred rupee note? By using it, by checking whether it can give him five hundred chocolates. How can we know whether the holy name of God is God Himself? By chanting, by checking whether it actually gives the peace and bliss that the presence of God brings. Similarly, how can we know whether the Deity is God Himself? By worshipping Him, by checking whether it actually brings the purification and satisfaction that contact with the all-pure, all-loving Supreme brings.

In the temples around the world, there are many sincere pujaris who have been unflinchingly serving their Deities for decades. They wake up very early in the morning, strictly follow the rules of cleanliness and purity and serve the Deity with scrupulous attention. And they do this day in and day out, month after month, year after year, decade after decade. How could they do this if they were not experiencing spiritual satisfaction and reciprocation from the Deities? No one can ever worship an idol like that. Their steadfast dedication is itself living proof of the presence of the Divine as the

Deities.

RG (*thoughtfully*)**:** You mean God has a form and that form is the same as the form of the Deity.

SS (*assertively*)**:** Certainly. If all of us are the children of God and we have a form, how can our Supreme Parent not have a form? Not only does God have a form, but He also has a form that is millions of times more attractive than any form of this world. Indeed, when our eyes relish the beauty of His form, then all worldly forms lose their charm and we fall completely in love with Him.

RG: But God is said to be all-pervading. Doesn't a form make God limited?

SS: Doesn't formlessness also limit God? If God's creation had form and God Himself did not have form, then God would be lesser than His creation. Then how could He be the Supreme? Among the various attributes that make a thing attractive, form is one of the most important, if not the most important. If God did not have form, then how could He be all-attractive?

Moreover, formlessness in itself does not make a thing unlimited. If someone destroys the form of a house by blowing it up, is the formless heap unlimited? No. What causes limitation is not form, but matter.
Matter is always limited, whether it is with form or without form. But God is spiritual and so is unlimited, whether with form or without form.

God being complete also has an impersonal aspect. The Srimad Bhagavatam (1.2.11) explains that the Absolute Truth manifests Himself in three aspects:

vadanti tat tattva vidas   tattvam yad jnanam advayam
brahmeti paramatemeti   bhagavan iti shabdyate

God manifests Himself as:

1. An all-pervading effulgence called the brahmajyoti which is like the sunlight coming from the sun

2. A localized expansion called the Paramatma

(Supersoul) who exists in the heart of every living entity and in every atom and who sustains the material cosmos.

3. An all-attractive Supreme Person called Bhagavan (the Supreme Personality of Godhead) who reciprocates love eternally with His devotees in His own spiritual abode.

This understanding that God is both personal and impersonal is the most complete understanding of the Absolute Truth and it is technically known as the achintyabhedabheda tattva (simultaneous oneness and difference).

RG (*after a long pause*)**:** This is quite convincing; it reconciles and integrates all that I have heard till now. A related question: I have heard people arguing that there is no need to go to a temple because, anyway, God is present everywhere. What do you have to say about that?

SS: This is a common excuse for shirking one's duty to God. Srila Prabhupada would give a simple refutation: God may be present everywhere, but can we experience

His presence everywhere? Water is present everywhere in the atmosphere as water vapor, but can we just stick out our tongue and take the water vapor whenever we feel thirsty. No, we have to go to a place where the water is made accessible to us – a tap. Similarly, if we want to purify ourselves and benefit from the presence of God, we need to go to a place where He is made accessible to us – the temple.

Now, I would like to ask you a question: Why do you think people come to the temple?

RG: Well, among the people I know who go to the temple, most of them always have some desire that they want fulfilled. Someone wants to pass an exam; someone wants to have a good spouse; someone wants his business to flourish. I always felt uneasy with this kind of worship; it seemed to be more like business and less like devotion to me. To be honest with you, that was why I would not visit temples much.

SS: I agree with your feeling. The Vedic scriptures state that the motives with which people come to God can be categorized into four major levels: fear, desire, duty and love.

1. Fear: People at this level think, "If I disobey God, then He may punish me for my wrongdoings. So better let me go to His temple and pacify Him by my worship." This sort of worship is certainly better than atheism, but it is based on a very negative conception of God as a stern judge, a cosmic punisher.

2. Desire: People at this level think, "There are so many things I want; if I pray to God, perhaps He will give them to me." Here the conception of God is more positive, as a potent desire-fulfiller, but still it is a highly utilitarian relationship based on give-and-take rather than love. Srila Prabhupada would say that if we go to God to ask for bread, then that shows our love for bread, not our love for God.

3. Duty: People at this level think, "God has already given me so much – life, body, health, food, clothing, shelter. It is my duty to go periodically to His temple and thank Him." Here the relationship is somewhat steady being based on gratitude for what has already been given and not on greed for what one wants to receive. Still, over time duty can become a burden. Moreover, the focus in this level

is still on what God has done for me, not on God Himself.

4. Love: This is the purest level of approaching God, where a devotee feels, "My dear Lord, you are the supreme object of my love; I have been offering my love to so many people and things, but that has never made me happy. Now I simply want to love and serve You eternally and I do not want anything material in return for my service; I simply wish to love You and to be loved by You. Just as a parent takes care of the child without the child having to ask his parents, similarly, I know that you will take care of me. I will accept whatever is Your plan for me and keep serving You no matter what happens in my material life."

The real purpose of going to a temple is not to have our desires *fulfilled*, but to have our desires *purified* so that we can rise to the level of love.

RG: This level of love sounds so sweet. Can you please tell me more about it?

SS (*enthusiastically*): Surely. In fact, fulfilling our longing for love is the next purpose served by the temple.

LOVE

SS: Just as food, clothing and shelter are the fundamental needs of the body, just as peace is the basic need of the mind, similarly love is the essential need of the soul. The Vedic texts assert that this loving propensity can be completely and eternally fulfilled only when it is directed to God. When a person has one or more of the six principal opulences – beauty, wealth, intelligence, strength, fame or renunciation, that person becomes attractive in our eyes. Being supreme by definition, God possesses all these cherished attributes in full eternally; He is thus supremely beautiful, supremely wealthy, supremely intelligent, supremely strong, supremely famous and supremely renounced. God has many names that refer to His different qualities, like Allah, Yahweh, Jehovah. But the cumulative result of all His qualities is that He is universally attractive and the name that describes Him best is the name that refers to His all-attractiveness. That name, according to the Vedic scriptures, is Krishna, which in Sanskrit means all-attractive. *sarva akarshati it krishna* "That Supreme Being who attracts everyone is known as Krishna." Over and above these six attractive qualities, Krishna also has an especially endearing seventh opulence – a most loving nature. In the spiritual realm, He personally and individually  reciprocates with the love of each soul. Krishna is thus the perfect object of love and the soul's longing for love, when reposed in Krishna, finds everlasting fulfillment.

RG: How do we develop our love for Krishna?

SS: The temple is the place where we experience Krishna's love for us and thus fulfill our hunger for love. The temple also gives us the opportunity to express our love for Krishna by rendering service and thus redirecting our love from matter to Krishna. How does the temple provide us experience of Krishna's love for us? Through His Deities, His philosophical teachings, His wonderful pastimes, His sweet holy names and especially His kind-hearted devotees.

Krishna loves all His children, even those children who have forgotten Him. So, just as an obedient son tries to please his father by getting a wayward brother back home, the devotees express their love for Krishna by carrying His message of love to the forgetful souls. Saintly persons from all religions have radiated this divine extraordinary love and thus inspired thousands to reciprocate and develop their dormant love for God. For example, when Jesus was being brutally crucified, he compassionately prayed for the well being of those who were torturing him, "Forgive them, O Lord, for they know not what they do." Similarly, Prahlad Maharaj prayed to the Lord for the deliverance of his demoniac father Hiranyakashipu, alhough his father had repeatedly tried to abuse, torment and kill him.

RG: Can this sort of divine love be seen in today's world?

SS: Certainly. Srila Prabhupada is an ideal example. He risked his life to go to America in old age, and tolerated sea sickness, heart attacks, robbery and murderous attacks. Why did he accept all these hardships? Simply out of love – love for Krishna and love for all of Krishna's children. When Srila Prabhupada was living in the bowery amidst the hippies, he would not just speak Bhagavad-gita to them; he would also cook for them, serve them prasad, even wash their plates after they left. Why was he doing all this for them? What was the relationship between him and them? Materially they could not have been more different; he was elderly, they were young; he was a distinguished Sanskrit and religious scholar, they were college dropouts; he was a clean, cultured gentleman, they were unclean, unkempt derelicts; he was a pure devotee, who had never known any bad habits throughout his life; they were rebellious addicts, habituated to meat-eating, intoxication, gambling and illicit sex. So the relationship between Srila Prabhupada and the hippies was spiritual; Srila Prabhupada saw them as beloved children of Krishna, who had a slight spark of interest in knowing about Krishna. So Srila Prabhupada did all he could to fan that spark and help them revive their innate love for Krishna.

Many of these hippies responded to Srila Prabhupada's selfless love and became so transformed and elevated that they themselves became carriers of divine love for others.

Why do we need a temple? 59

RG: Srila Prabhupada's saintliness and selfless love are so heart-rending to hear about.

SS: Yes, the devotees' love for us gives us a glimpse of Krishna's love for us. And the primary way the devotees express their love for us is by helping us develop our love for Krishna. The Bhagavad-gita describes Krishna as our *suhrda*, our eternal well-wisher, our ultimate heart-to-heart friend. And devotees who help us to revive our forgotten relationship with Krishna are also our true friends. Srila Prabhupada would tell a story to illustrate how a devotee does the best welfare work for others.

Suppose you are the friend of a very wealthy person. One day you see your friend's estranged son wandering like a vagabond on the streets, drunk, disheveled, diseased, distressed and starving. Somebody comes and offers him some food. He hungrily gulps down the food and continues his aimless wandering. Then someone else comes and offers him a new set of clothes. He happily wears the clothes, but still remains lost and forsaken. Then someone else gives him

a few free medicines, which offer him some physical relief, but don't give any permanent solace. Then you take him home in your car, and arrange for his bathing, food and treatment. When he has sobered down, you talk with him lovingly and explain to him his father's great affection and longing for him. Then you clarify and remove the misunderstanding that had strained his relationship with his father. And when he is ready to return back to his father, you take him back to his father's mansion where he is given the best varieties of foods, offered an entire wardrobe of clothes and attended to by a team of expert doctors. Thus you have helped solve his problems permanently.

Similarly, all of us are beloved children of the Supreme Lord, who is the Master of the Goddess of Fortune. Therefore we are all like princes in the kingdom of God. But due to our misuse of our free will, we have left the shelter of our all-loving father and are struggling for paltry pleasure in this material world, exactly like the lost son of that wealthy man. The material welfare workers are like the people who offered food, clothing and medicine to the lost son, whereas the devotee is like the father's friend who took the son back to his father.

RG: Beautiful story.

SS: The temple is the place where we can come in touch with devotees who lead us back to our eternal home. So in one sense the temple is a pointer to our eternal home, but in a deeper, spiritual sense, the temple *is* our eternal home.

RG: Really? How is that?

SS: Krishna is so concerned about our well being that He constantly beckons us from within our hearts to return home. To make His invitation more appealing and realistic, He even manifests His abode here in this world. To understand how that's possible, let's analyze the phrase "the kingdom of God", which is another way of referring to the spiritual world.

Is the kingdom of God restricted to some remote, inaccessible corner of existence? Is God not the king of all parts of existence? Then is the kingdom of God not everywhere?

It is – and is not.

Everywhere is indeed the kingdom of God, but

everywhere He is not acknowledged as the king. So, that part of existence where He is not only acknowledged, but also loved, as the king is specially called in the scriptures as the kingdom of God.

And that same kingdom of God manifests itself at all those places – like temples –where God is genuinely accepted and glorified as the king. That's why most people – even nonbelievers – who visit a temple experience a mystical calm, an inexplicable peace. Though they may not understand, that peace is a glimpse of the joy of homecoming; for the temple subconsciously reminds them of their eternal home.

Kings of ancient India would glorify God as the king of all kings by building His temples bigger than their own palaces. That's why we need big, beautiful temples today too: to attract people to visit and thus discover the way to their eternal home.

And the temple is a home in another sense; all the devotees connected with a temple, because of their common aspiration of loving Krishna, become like one extended family. And the temple becomes the common home for this large family. ISKCON temples have a weekly Sunday program where all the devotees come together; at that time, the joy among the devotees is just like the joy during a family get-together. And the amazing thing about this family is that it has  members from different states, castes, nations, religions all united together lovingly in service to Krishna. That's why it is said about Srila Prabhupada that "he built a house in which the whole world can live." •

RG: The temple as a university, then as a hospital, now as a home – this is an amazing presentation of the contribution of the temple to society… Talking about contribution to society, when we develop our love for Krishna, how does that affect our love for those immediately related to us like our family members?

SS: It is only when we love Krishna that we can truly love others – including our family members. The more people neglect or reject God, the more their view of life and family becomes materialistic and they see their family members as nothing but facilitators for their enjoyment. When they stop getting the desired enjoyment from their family members, they dump them as fast as they would dump a broken down TV. No wonder that with the increase in godlessness and materialism, joint families have disintegrated into nuclear families. And sadly now nuclear families are breaking into solitary protons and neutrons wandering aimlessly in search of love. The Bollywood idea of love is very superficial; nowadays men and women say that they love each other, but actually men treat women like sex machines and women treat men like ATM machines.

RG (*smiling*)**:** That's a humorous way of portraying a harsh reality.

SS: But that harsh reality can be changed. When we put God at the center of our hearts and families, then we see our family members as representatives of God in our life and we naturally serve them with respect and love instead of using them for our purposes.

Moreover, when our hearts are devoted to God, then God uses us as His instruments to express His infinite love for all His children. When we become carriers of divine love, our expressions of love fully satisfy the hearts of our loved ones. In an ideal family, the vertical relationship with God and the horizontal relationships among the family members reinforce each other. Our vertical relationship makes us more tolerant and service-oriented in our horizontal relationships and our horizontal relationships become means for us to serve Krishna and thus develop our vertical relationship. Thus, the temple helps us develop our love not only for Krishna, but also for our family members.

RG (*thoughtfully*)**:** Makes sense. But isn't it also true that some people give up their family responsibilities due to their devotion to God? In your temple, you have so many young brahmacharis who have given up their duties to their parents.

SS: Firstly, there are not so many brahmacharis; as compared to the total number of ISKCON devotees, the brahmacharis will be just about one percent.

Secondly, we make sure they don't just give up their duties, but rather complete their basic family responsibilities. They help arrange for their sisters' marriages, they repay their family loans, they arrange for the future financial security of their parents. Only then do we allow them to join as brahmacharis.

Thirdly, they are not actually giving up duties; rather they are taking up higher duties, in fact, the highest human duty of purifying one's heart and developing one's love for Krishna. Only when people see living  examples of purity and devotion will they be inspired to pursue those goals themselves. The brahmacharis strive to become such examples by leading a life of simplicity and austerity, waking up daily latest by 4 am and engaging in rigorous spiritual practices.

RG (*amazed*)**:** All the brahmacharis wake up by 4 am?

SS: Yes, the brahmacharis participate in the morning program without fail. At 4:30 am, the Deities offer Their first darshan of the day and the devotees worship Them by performing mangala arti. The artis and kirtans continue till 5:30 am. Then from 5:30 am to 7:30 am, the devotees chant japa. Then at 7:30 am, the Deities after being bathed, dressed and decorated, offer darshan again, after which we have guru-puja. Then we have class on the Srimad Bhagavatam till around 9 am. During the day, the brahmacharis render various services in the temple. And in the evenings, they go out to conduct programs in different parts of the city. In this way, by living a life centered on Krishna, they develop their love for Krishna and share that love with others.

Fourthly, even from a social point of view, the brahmacharis take up higher duties, duties so vital and valuable that they leave no time for other duties. They leave a small family to make the whole of humanity their family and work tirelessly for the welfare of thousands of people. Earlier, we discussed how the temple is like a university. The brahmacharis are like the professors in the university. Today spiritual education is so desperately needed in society, so many people are living aimless, misdirected lives and so few teachers are available to show them the way. Being unconstrained by family demands, the brahmacharis use their purified intelligence and youthful energy to share spiritual wisdom far and wide. Earlier we discussed how the temple is like a hospital administering medication to sick minds. Well, the brahmacharis are the full-time doctors in that hospital. There are so many spiritually sick people, there is such a great need for spiritually qualified doctors and the brahmacharis are the few gallant souls who take up the noble cause of treating the sick.

And lastly, we never force anyone to become a brahmachari; in fact, we test their inspiration and determination by making them aware of the challenges of life in the renounced order. Only those rare souls who are inspired to dedicate their lives to a glorious cause take up the challenge of becoming a fulltime spiritual teacher. In Vedic culture, those who would sacrifice their lives to teach God's message to society were considered glorious, just as now those who sacrifice their lives to join the army and defend the country are considered glorious. Initially, the parents are upset when their sons leave them, but over the years when they see their son's pure, noble lifestyle and his committed service to humanity, they start appreciating what he is doing and even start practicing devotional service themselves.

RG: Oh, I had no idea of the services that the brahmacharis were rendering to God and humanity.

Certainly, from what I have seen, the brahmacharis look quite spirited, happy and active.

SS (*smiling*): Yes, the temple has so much to do to share God's love with society and they are the main people doing most of the services. That brings us to the last contribution of the temple.

ENGAGEMENT

SS: Srila Prabhupada was the first spiritual teacher who translated "bhakti" not just as "devotion", but as "devotional service". He did this to counter the prevailing misconception that bhakti is just a matter of the heart, a notion that is often used for shirking from doing anything practical for serving God. Certainly, bhakti is a matter of the heart, but what is in the heart is expressed in one's words and in one's actions and in one's very life. When a mother loves her child, she serves the child by cooking a delicacy for him.

Similarly, we should express our love for Krishna by serving Him, by doing something wonderful and pleasing for Him. Therefore Srila Prabhupada also wrote, "Devotional service is not a matter of sentimental speculation or imaginative ecstasy. Its substance is practical activity."

RG: Interesting. So what sort of practical activity does devotional service involve?

SS: By engaging whatever we have – our talents and resources, our intelligence and our energy – in serving Krishna. One important way to render service to Krishna is by building a majestic temple for Him. That's why in Vedic culture, the kings would consider it an honor to have the opportunity to build a temple for the Lord. Sometimes, a temple would be so  magnificent that several generations of successive kings would build it over centuries.

RG: I have seen some medieval temples during my

tours of South India; they are artistic and architectural marvels.

SS: Yes. The essential principle of devotional service is that our love will be seen when we offer Krishna the very best that we can. So, as per his capacity, the king would offer the Lord a grand temple. Others would offer their best as per their capacity. For example, in Vedic culture, the artists would utilize their artistic talents to glorify the Lord. Through drama, dance, music, painting, sculpture, the artists would depict the pastimes of Krishna, thus flooding their audience's hearts with devotional emotions. Thus everyone – the artists, the patrons and the audience – would experience the purifying remembrance of Krishna and thus joyfully advance in God consciousness.

But sadly this glorious culture is dying in India. With the advent of TV, movies and internet, many children are not even aware of the basics of their culture. Recently, I was invited to give a talk

in a school. When I asked the children whether they had heard of Lord Narasimhadeva, they replied that they had heard only of Narasimha Rao. It's heartbreaking that these children, despite being born in India, are not receiving the immense inspiration and deep wisdom that our rich culture has to offer.

RG (*sadly*)**:** I know. With nuclear families, there are no grandparents to tell traditional stories to their children. And often both parents are working and so they have no time.

SS (*brightening up*)**:** But Srila Prabhupada worked tirelessly to revive the Vedic culture not only in India but all over the world. In Vedic society, the temple was like the cultural capital. So if we start with a vibrant temple, then the culture will radiate outwards to the whole society from there. And that's exactly happening in many ISKCON temples. For example, in our temple, we have an active drama team comprising of children, youth and congregation devotees. These amateur artists perform skits and plays on Janmashtami and other festivals depicting the Lord's pastimes.

RG: I attended a Janmashtami festival at an ISKCON

temple, where there was a beautiful drama about the birth of Lord Krishna. The devotional mood was moving.

SS: Yes. When the dramas are performed by devotees, their devotion invokes the dormant devotion in the hearts of the audience. That devotional transformation does not happen if the drama is enacted by paid professionals, even if their performance is better artistically.

The dramas are just one part of the cultural revival. Festivals at ISKCON are nowadays becoming like a cultural bonanza with Bharatnatyam performances, gorgeous decorations of the Deities, beautification of the temple premises and captivating dioramas depicting the pastimes related with the festivals. During festivals, thousands of people crowd the temples for darshan. Despite the inconveniences caused by crowding, everyone is visibly joyful, because their hearts are enlivened; they are experiencing divine love.

RG: I often wondered what made people go to temples and on pilgrimages despite so many bodily inconveniences. Now I am beginning to understand;

their spiritual joy takes their mind off their bodily inconvenience.

SS: Exactly.

RG: You were talking about the devotional culture in ancient India and you mentioned how the kings and the artists rendered service. But what about those who are not so wealthy or so talented? How would they be spiritually engaged?

SS: Those who are not endowed with any special gifts can do for Krishna whatever they are doing in their daily lives. That's why Lord Krishna says in the Bhagavad-gita (9.27),

yat karoshi yad ashnasi   yaj juhosi dadasi yat

yat tapasyasi kaunteya   tat kurushva mad-arpanam

"Whatever you do, whatever you eat, whatever you offer or give away, and whatever austerities you perform—do that as an offering to Me." This verse is a vivid expression of God's love for us and His eagerness to make our way back to Him as easy as possible. When we live in the material world, we all do some activities to fulfill our worldly duties. If we just do those very same activities for Krishna, then Krishna accepts those activities as expressions of our bhakti for Him. For example,

- A DTP professional can help format the posters and pamphlets about Krishna's festivals.

- A marketing professional can assist in distributing Krishna's books so that His message of divine love can reach more and more people.

- A professor or teacher can share Krishna's teachings from the Gita in addition to teaching his academic subjects.

- A businessman who is expert in financial dealings can help raise funds for Krishna's temple.

- A software professional can help set up the computer systems required for efficient management of Krishna's temples.

- A housewife who cooks for her family can help cook for the Deities in the temple.

- A child who learns storytelling in school can learn and tell stories of Krishna's adventurous pastimes.

In this way, the temple offers everyone some practical way to engage in devotional service and thus make spiritual advancement.

RG: This devotional culture is very inclusive; it seems the only qualification is the desire. If someone wants to serve the Lord, there are many ways open for him.

SS: Yes. And there are two ways in which practically everyone can serve the Lord.

RG: What are they?

SS: The first is by eating.

RG (*surprised*)**:** Eating?

SS: Yes. All of us have to eat to live. If before eating our food, we just offer the food to Krishna with devotion,

Krishna accepts our devotion and, by His mercy, transforms the food into Prasad. Taking prasad is a very essential and joyful way of serving the Lord.

RG: Now I understand. In many other temples, prasad is a morsel of sweet food that one gets. But in ISKCON temples, the full meal is called prasad. If I understand right, any food that is offered to the Lord becomes prasad.

SS: Perfect. In fact, serious devotees don't eat any food that is not offered to the Lord. Prasad is delicious and purifying. We try our best to ensure that every visitor who comes to the temple gets at least some prasad.

RG: Yes, I have seen the counter just outside the temple where the visitors get a cup of sweet. What is the other way of serving the Lord?

SS: Charity. The principle of devotional service is to give our heart to Krishna. But often that is not easy to do because our heart is already given to so many other people and things. Therefore we should offer to Krishna those things where our heart is. By so doing, we offer a part of our heart to Krishna, or, in other words, we allow Krishna to enter a part of our heart. For most of us, our heart is in our earnings. So by offering a part of our earnings to Krishna, we are actually giving Krishna a place in our heart.

The amount of charity can be according to our means, but the guiding principle is that we are offering our heart and our love to Krishna. If we loved someone deeply and wanted to give that person a gift, we would give the best that we could, not give some useless or leftover item from the household junk. Similarly, if we are serious about our relationship with Krishna, we will offer Him the best that we can.

RG: This is a new way of thinking for me. I have not seen many people who think so seriously in terms of a relationship with God. Changing the topic slightly, I have noticed that ISKCON is not only reviving the traditional culture, but is also using a lot of modern gadgetry.

SS: Yes, that is the application of the Vedic principle called yukta-vairagya: "Without personal attachment, one should use everything for Krishna's service." A devotee understands that the whole world belongs to

Krishna. So a devotee does not renounce the world; rather he engages the whole world in Krishna's service. As people are attracted by hi-tech displays, a devotee uses technology to depict Krishna's teachings and pastimes, and thus attract people to Krishna. For example,

- ISKCON is constructing splendid temples equipped with state-of-the-art animatronics, robotics and multimedia theaters to kindle the interest of people in the message of the Bhagavad-Gita.

- At many of ISKCON's major festivals, sophisticated lasers shows offer breathtaking glimpses of beautiful Deities being worshiped all over the world and thus inspire devotion among the people.

- ISKCON is offering children devotionally-oriented toys, games and movies, which foster virtue and nobility, as a positive alternative to the current trend of entertainment that features violence and sensuality and breeds vice.

- ISKCON's faculty members give presentations using slides shows, VCDs, LCD projectors, laptops and other state-of-the-art technology.

This spiritual utilization of technology is attracting millions of people towards the service of God, and helping them to find inner fulfillment and achieve their right to eternal life and happiness.

Thus, in ISKCON, we have modernization without westernization; we accept the modern gadgets, but not the western materialism.

RG: Modernization without westernization! That's exactly what India needs today.

SS: Yes. In fact, Srila Prabhupada went even further. He envisioned a grand East-West synthesis: spreading Indian spiritual wisdom by using Western material technology. He compared the coming together of Vedic spirituality and modern technology to the coming together of the proverbial blind man and the lame man. But for this synthesis to take place, the technologically advanced West has to recognize that it is lacking in spiritual vision. And the financially-crippled India has to shed its deeply-ingrained inferiority complex arising from material poverty and recognize its wealth of spiritual knowledge. Srila Prabhupada was one Indian who fully recognized India's unnoticed wealth and wanted to share it with the whole world. Thus when he went to USA, he told the Americans that he had come not to take, but to give. When a flippant British reporter asked Srila Prabhupada on his arrival in London, "What is the purpose of your visit?" Srila Prabhupada eloquently replied, "When you British ruled India, you plundered India of all her wealth. But you forgot to take the most precious jewel of India. I have come to give you what you forgot to take – the devotional wisdom of India."

Following in Srila Prabhupada's footsteps, ISKCON devotees are working tirelessly at the grassroots level all over the world to bring about the East-West synthesis. When the new temple comes up, it will be a significant step forward in the integration of the ancient India with the modern India and in the holistic development of our great country.

So let me recap the answer to your question about the need for a big temple:

T. Tranquility of the temple offers essential

refreshing breaks that empower people to face the stresses of life. To get similar breaks, many people seek entertainment, which is an industry costing millions. When we don't object to the money spent on arranging for that sort of breaks, then why object to money being spent on arranging for spiritual breaks that offer similar and arguably better refreshment?

E. Education provided by the temple helps people lead a life of moral and spiritual integrity, which is the basis that enables people to use all their other education for socially beneficial purposes. When we consider establishing new universities for material education as a sign of national progress, then why not similarly celebrate the building of a university for spiritual education?

M. Medication provided by the temple can heal the diseased mentality that impels people to addiction and criminality, both of which cause an enormous drain on the national economy. If we recognize as a social necessity the building of hospitals that heal the body, then why not similarly recognize as a social necessity the erection of hospitals that heal the mind?

P. Purification that the temple offers can train talented people to become pure-hearted, selfless, principle-centered leaders. When leaders with character are acutely needed in every organization from the family to the government, then why not welcome an institute that can produce high quality leaders?

L. Love that the temple inspires in people can provide them deep satisfaction and dramatically improve their relationships. When relationship conflicts are causing unprecedented misery in society, they why not support an institution that can provide a solid foundation for lasting relationships?

E. Engagements offered by the temple help preserve our national culture, and also productively channelize people's talents and energies. When our national culture is being lost at an alarming rate, then why not help a forum that is not only protecting but also reviving it?

And if one institution can offer all these six benefits simultaneously, why should we not participate and rejoice in its establishment? The bigness of the temple is not a gaudy luxury, but a functional necessity; it has big roles to play, big services to offer. For example, to serve as an effective university for spiritual education, it needs seminar halls, conference rooms and libraries. To serve as a vibrant cultural center that can properly serve the thousands of people who crowd it on festivals, it needs a large temple hall, a large prasad hall and a large pravachan (discourse) hall.

To conclude, I would like to thank you, Guptaji, for investing so much of your time and thought in this long discussion. The world would be a much better place if we had more people with your level of social concern and spiritual interest.

RG: It is I who should thank you, Swamiji. To say the very least, this has been the most enlightening discussion I have ever had in my life. I will surely do all that I can to help in building the new temple and will also try to get my friends to help.

SS: If you do that, you will receive eternal blessings from Lord Krishna and you will also benefit the whole society. Thank you very much. Hare Krishna.

Ratan Gupta offers his respects to Swamiji and takes

leave. As Ratan is about to enter his car, he turns to have a last look at the temple. He sees, in the distance, the dignified figure of Swamiji seated behind his desk, studying what looks like an ancient book. As he reflects, he is amazed at how much he has learnt in the last few hours and how it has given him a whole new outlook towards a temple and towards life in general.

Acknowledgements

The first and foremost acknowledgements for this book are due to His Grace Radheshyam Prabhu, my spiritual mentor and principal shiksha-guru, who inspired me to focus on this book among all other writing projects, gave vital feedback to help refine the manuscript and also suggested the cover page idea.

I thank my beloved spiritual master, His Holiness Radhanath Maharaj, whose autobiography has become the compass of my writing and my life.

His Holiness Jayadvaita Maharaj, my "writing guru", has persistently invested his time to train me in writing, despite my being an incredibly lazy student. I hope, somewhat nervously, that this book – my first attempt at writing in a conversational format – will pass his quality control tests.

When all hopes of publishing this book within the required deadline seemed lost, Sripad Prabhu made the impossible possible by taking up full responsibility for designing the cover page, overseeing the formatting of the book and dealing with the printer. My special thanks to him and his competent and dedicated team comprising of Boldsukh Prabhu, Chandrakrishna Prabhu and other devotees.

A unique devotee-friend helped bring literary flavor to a crude manuscript by his scrutinizing editing. His desire for anonymity and my desire to acknowledge him are in conflict. As before, he wins.

Abhijit Toley Prabhu amazes me by his commitment to literary services despite having a demanding company job. His proofreading, editing and research helped refine the book.

Manish Vithalani Prabhu, my unfailing aid for research and my unfailing critic for writing, surprised me by his appreciation of this book.

Swaminathan Prabhu proofread the book and also offered thoughtful suggestions.

Many others including Balagovinda Prabhu, Padmalochan Prabhu, Shuka Priya Prabhu, Kundan Prabhu, Nitin Mehendale Prabhu and Venkata Buddhiraju Prabhu helped in ways that perhaps only a writer can understand.

My sincere thanks to them all.

Chaitanya Charan Das
Spiritual Mentor
VOICE, Pune

Books Published by

Vedic Oasis for Inspiration, Culture & Education (VOICE)

'Spirituality for the Modern Youth' series
- Discover Yourself
- Your Best Friend
- Your Secret Journey
- Victory Over Death
- Yoga of Love

Pocket Books
- Art of Mind Control
- Practical Tips to Mind Control
- Can I Live Forever?
- Do We Live More Than Once?
- Tryst With Eternal Beauty
- Recession – Adversity or Opportunity?
- Why Do We Need a Temple?

Other Books
- Essence of Bhagavad Gita Vol-1
- Essence of Bhagavad Gita Vol-2
- Essence of Bhagavad Gita Vol-3

- Essence of Bhagavad Gita Vol-4
- Youth Preaching Manual
- Bhagavad-gita 7 day Course
- Value Education

Children's Books:
- My First Krishna Book
- Getting to Know Krishna
- More About Krishna
- Devotees of Krishna
- Wonderful Krishna
- Krishna's Childhood Pastime

Spiritual Scientist series:
- The Spiritual Scientist Vol I
- The Spiritual Scientist Vol II
- Science and Spirituality

'Bring out the LEADER in you' series

Ideal for college students as well as corporate executives, this series of books will help them tap their latent qualities. The first two books in this series are already published and the remaining will soon be published.

- Stress Management
- ENERGY – Your Sutra for Positive Thinking
- Time Management

- Art of Self Management
- Power of Habits
- Secret of Concentration
- Mind your Mind
- Team playing & winning trust of others
- Overcoming Inferiority complex
- Constructive criticism – How to give it or take it?
- Fate and Free will
- Karma – the Law of Infallible justice
- Key to Real Happiness
- Conflict Resolution
- Eight Qualities of an Effective Leader
- Managing our Anger
- Self Development
- Personality development and Character buildup
- Proactive Leadership
- Art of Living and Leaving

For a free subscription to our ezine, please register a www.thespiritualscientist.com

Made in the USA
Lexington, KY
06 April 2017